Seaway

sea chants of poetry to navigate the way

Poetry by Savannah Green

Illustrations by Grace Spivey

ISBN: 978-0-578-91473-2
Independently Published by A Common Thread
Poetry by Savannah Green
Illustrations by Grace Spivey
Book cover by Kevin Ortega

DEDICATION

For all the aspiring writers – pour your coffee, grab your pen, and
keep writing.

For all the aspiring painters – pour your tea, grab your brush, and
keep painting.

Table of Contents

 1 Treasure Trove   2
 2 The Common Thread   4
 3 The Woods   6
 4 Annie   8
 5 Little Jean   10
 6 Kindred   12
 7 Boardwalk   14
 8 On the Brink   16
 9 Patch   18
10 Anchor   18
11 Reflecting Pool   20
12 Our Generation's Foundation   22
13 Bridges   24
14 At My Side   26
15 The Grass on My Path   28
16 Sea Glass   30
17 Taboo   32
18 Kindred Reprise   34
19 Oasis   36
20 Fly Little Jean Fly   38

- Poetry by Grace Spivey -
- Illustration by Savannah Green -

21 Floor of Stories   40
22 Seaway   42

ACKNOWLEDGMENTS

We are always grateful for our friends, families, and teachers who have encouraged us in our writing and painting. Without our communities, this book would not be in your hands right now. Thank you to those who kept this a secret along with us from the beginning and thank you to every reader who will now delve into this creative project. We put ourselves into this book, but we hope you see a way to find yourself in Seaway.

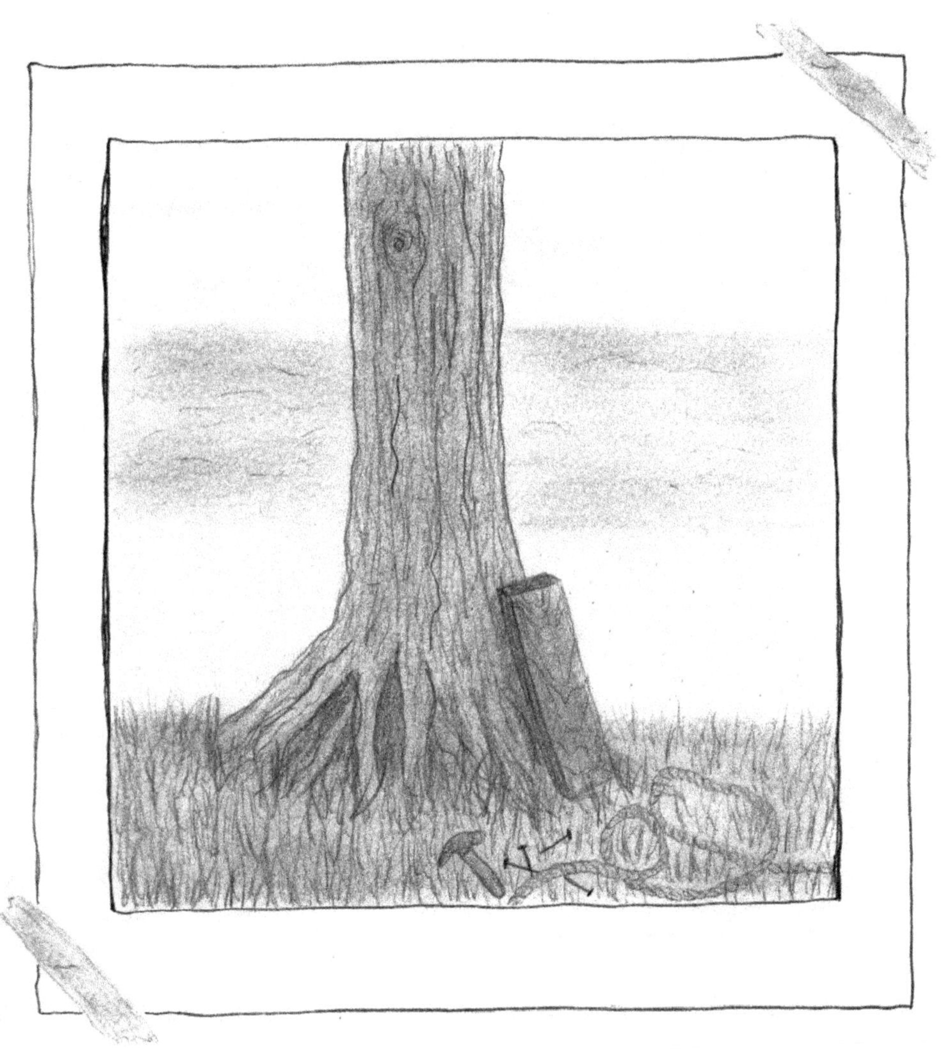

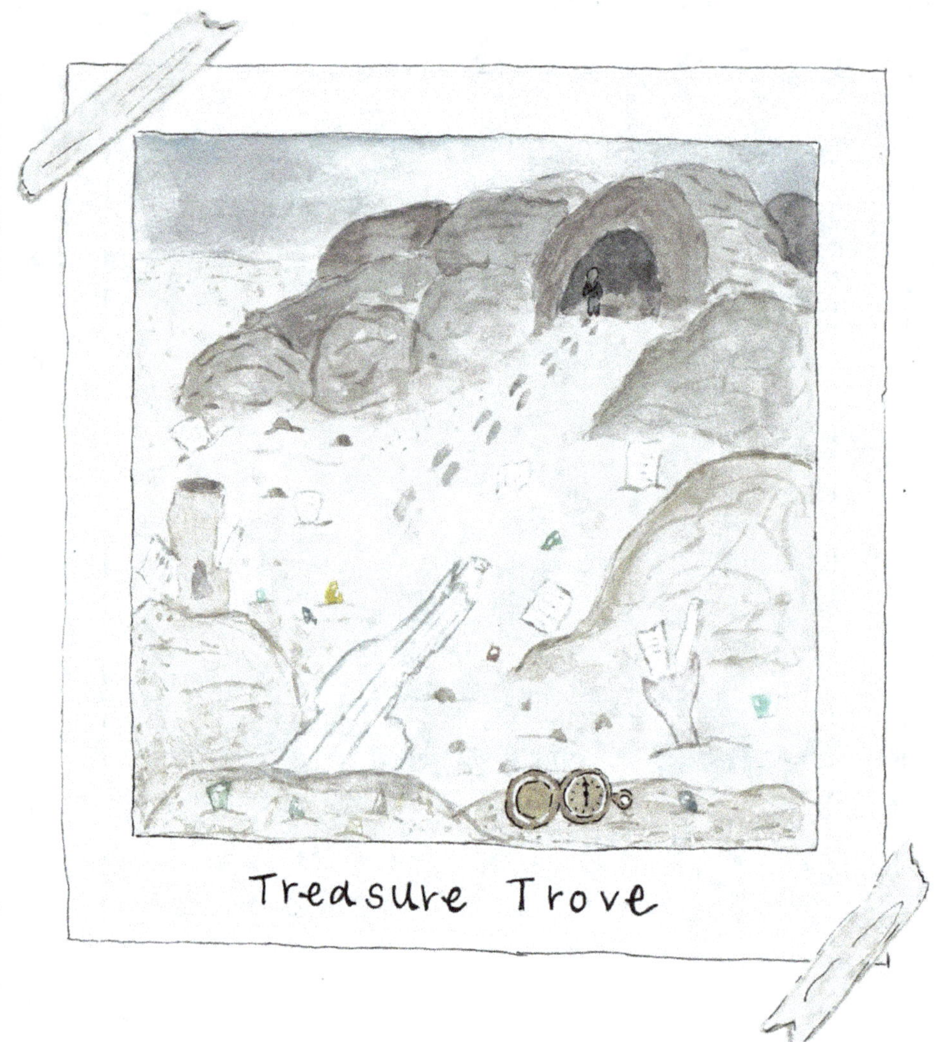

Treasure Trove

Treasure Trove

Verse 1
When the lights are dimmed
And I'm deep in my mind
I find peace within
One glow in the night

Twisted truths of deception
Unattainable expectations
Are overshadowed by
Contentment in imperfection

Chorus
Found in my golden treasure trove
Of unspoken pathos, unsung melodies, and unfinished prose
My collection I can dive in
With my dependable muse
A haven I can call my own
My one known

Verse 2
Insecurities undistinguishable
As the line where the ocean meets the sky
It makes it quite magical
In this peaceful cavern of mine

Fragile perceptions and assumptions of others
Are the sea glass pieces I've discovered
That are the best inspirations

Chorus

Bridge
Uncertainties crowned with assurance
A story without an end
Written down in sincere confidence
Held together by a pen
I cope with the unknown
Clinging to my one known

Chorus

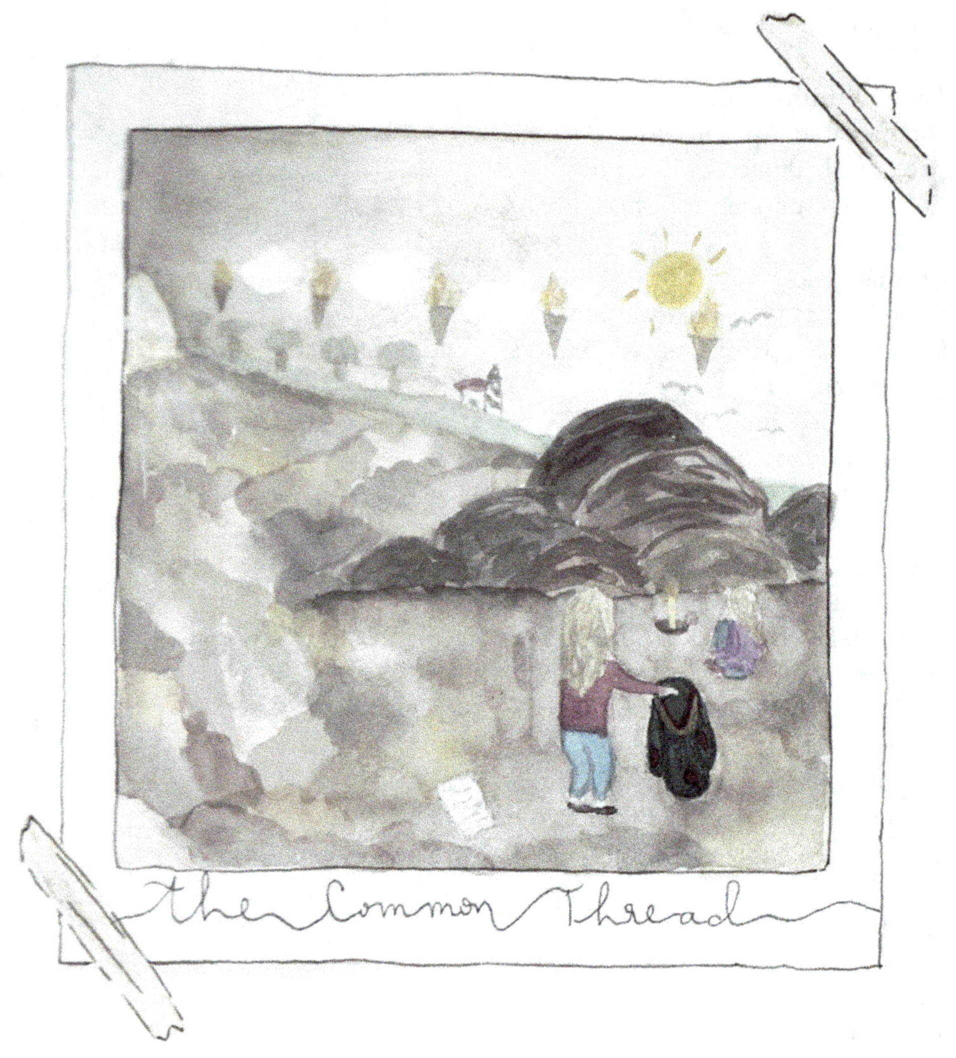

the Common Thread

The Common Thread

Verse 1
Memories of the years
Dance in my mind
All the truths I've learned
Over time

Verse 2
Bonds made of friendship
With gleaming grins and belly laughs
Through life's storms and trials
Have proven to last

Verse 3
A collection formed by
Paper and pen
Turned into treasured worth
From what's within

Verse 4
The Common Thread
I knitted in my sweater
Is what I pulled at my side
Through the years, now holding it together

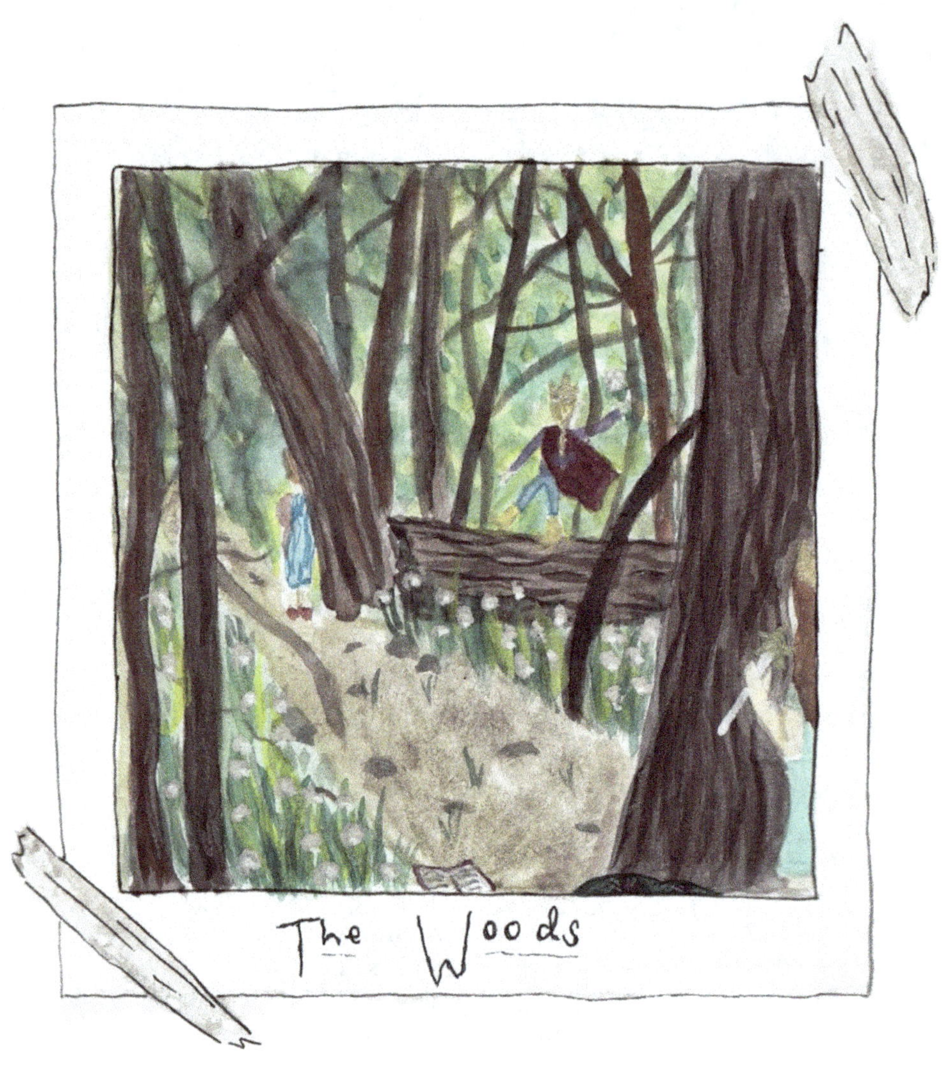

The Woods

The Woods

Verse 1
Prancing into the woods
For a game of hide 'n seek
Counting and trying not to peek

We run to grab our scripts
Dress in costumes and get ready
To put on a play for our family

Chorus
I fall asleep
Beneath the trees
With sweetest dreams
Always knowing
I'll wake up in the morning
To the world at my feet

Verse 2
I go about my day
As if it's a storybook
Humming to the singing brook
We walk along the rocks

And pick a bouquet of flowers
In the woods we made ours

Chorus

Bridge
With twigs in my braid
And mud on my cheeks
In these woods we made
Our masterpiece

At night our parents say
"Off to bed you go."
But we stay up
Pretending we're superheroes

Forever young
Never growing old
Memories one by one
Will one day be told

Chorus

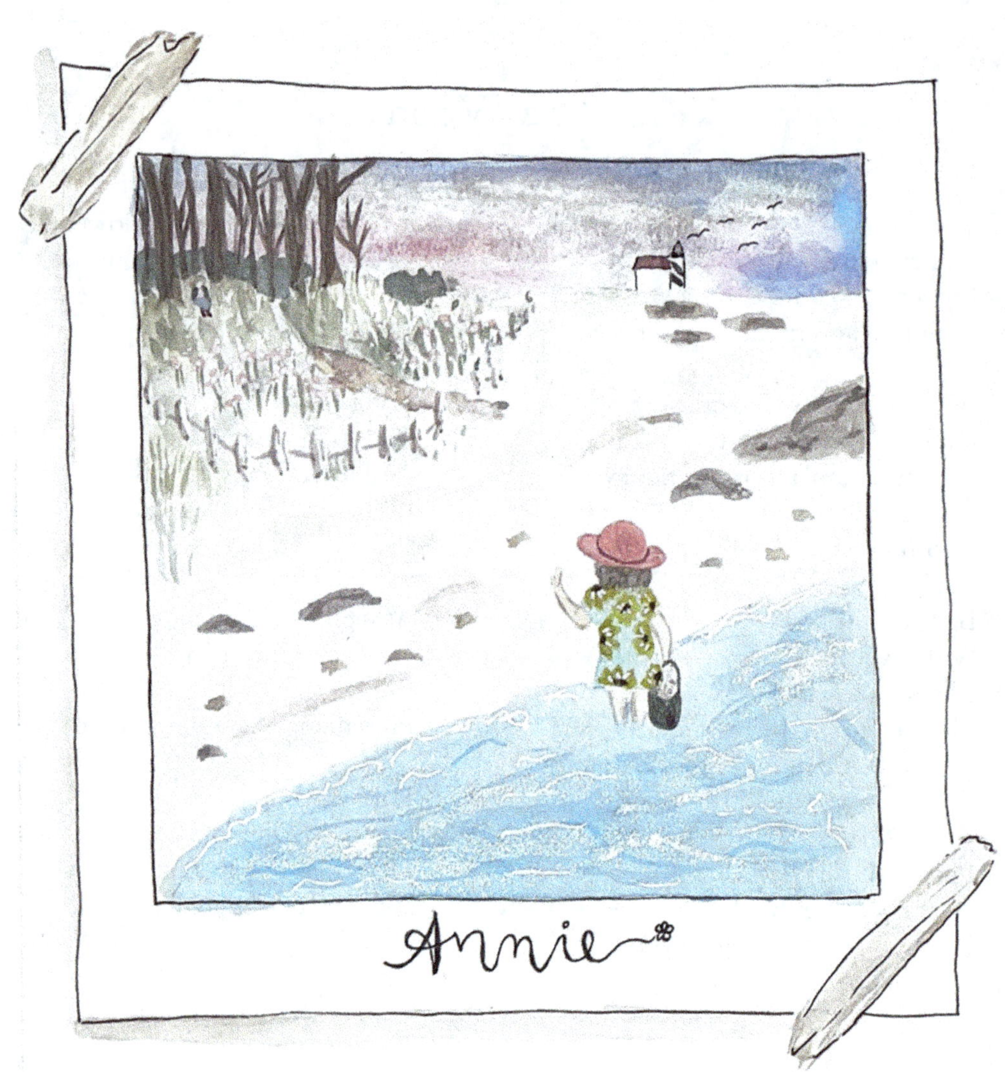

Annie

Annie

Verse 1
Your daddy wanted a baby boy
So he rolled his eyes
When he got a girl named Annie
Growing up as the youngest of five
Learning to make the most of life

Your crush gave you every quarter
From coin tosses at his football
games
You lost them all, wishing you'd
hid them better
But you were his Annie
So he married you on the
nineteenth of February

Chorus 1
Oh Annie, little do you know
There isn't one soul who
Doesn't want to be you
Oh Annie, I hope you know
Your sass is why others adore you
And your quiet spirit shines in all
you do

Verse 2
You raised three kids and made a
home
On a street named Dunn
Watched gardens and crops grow
Got blessed with five grandkids
And bragged on all they did

You watched as your family played
games
At every Christmas
And made sure everybody had a
place
On the family beach trip you spent
all your time
Looking for the best shells you
could find

Chorus 2
Oh Annie, what a beautiful name
And how special it's one others
love to say
For your presence makes for a
wonderful time
Whether there are laughs, tears, or
big ol' smiles
Oh Annie, you make life
worthwhile

Bridge
If you were still here
I'd share my writing
And you'd read it
And be proud
But you wouldn't dote on
My strivings and successes
My talents and achievements
You'd read my poetry
But be proud of me

Chorus 3
Oh Annie, little do you know
In everything I do
I just want to be like you
Oh Annie, I hope you know
I got your sass, but it looked better
on you
And I'm trying to have a quiet
spirit too

Oh Annie, what a beautiful name
And how special that it found a
place
Right in the middle of mine
Thinking of you brings laughs,
tears, and big ol' smiles
Oh Granny, you made life
worthwhile

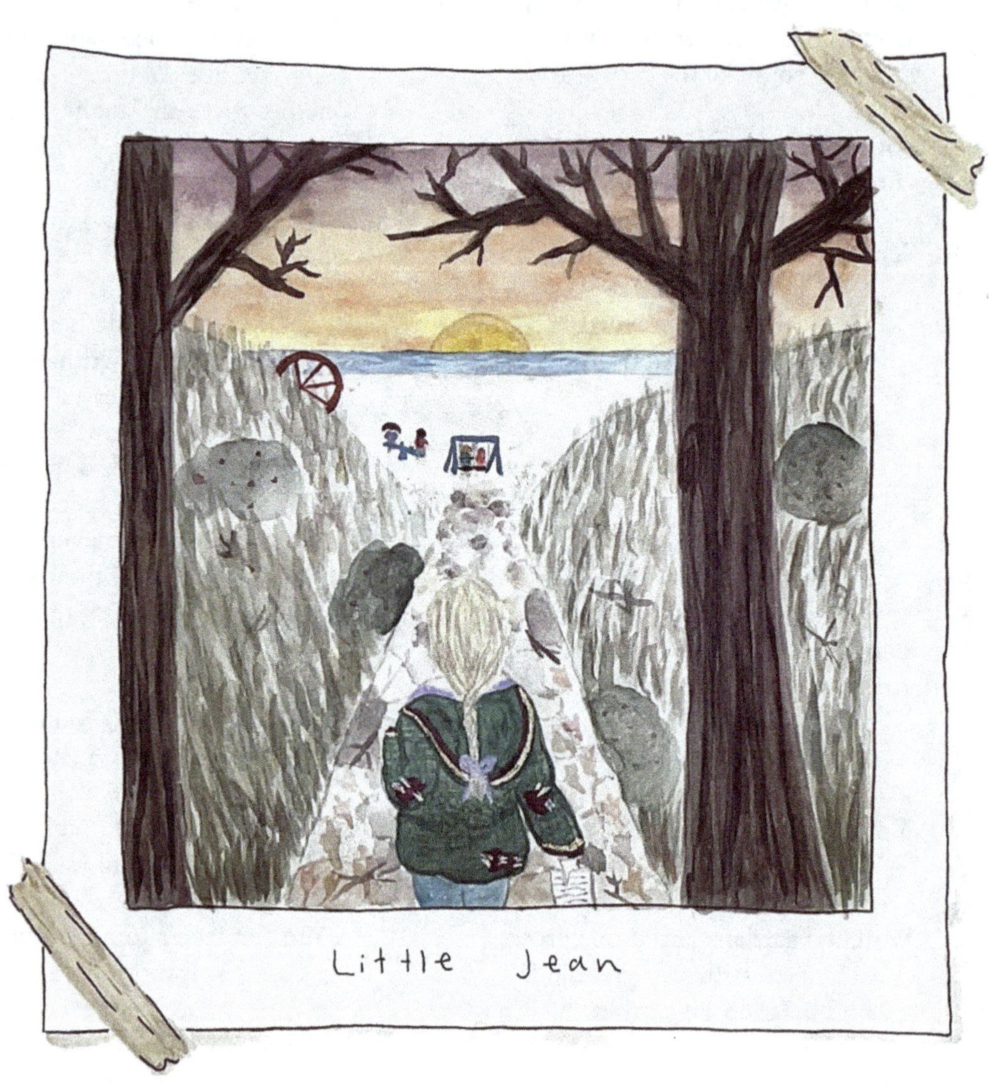

Little Jean

Little Jean

Verse 1
Dear Little Jean
What I'd give for you to see
Your imagination and daydreams
Make for more fun
So who cares they didn't save a spot
On the swings

Dear Little Jean
Your freckles sweetly sing
The song of the sun as it beams
On you in your backyard
Playing in your secret spot
A favorite place to be

Chorus
So keep painting beautiful skies
On the tapestry in your mind
The way you envelop
Waves of passion
The world you develop
From a single emotion
It's a treasure others yearn to find
Uniquely made, piece by piece
Made to be Little Jean

Verse 2
Dear Little Jean
One day you will see
You chase your dreams
Because you're brave
And have it in you
With a spot saved on the swings

Chorus

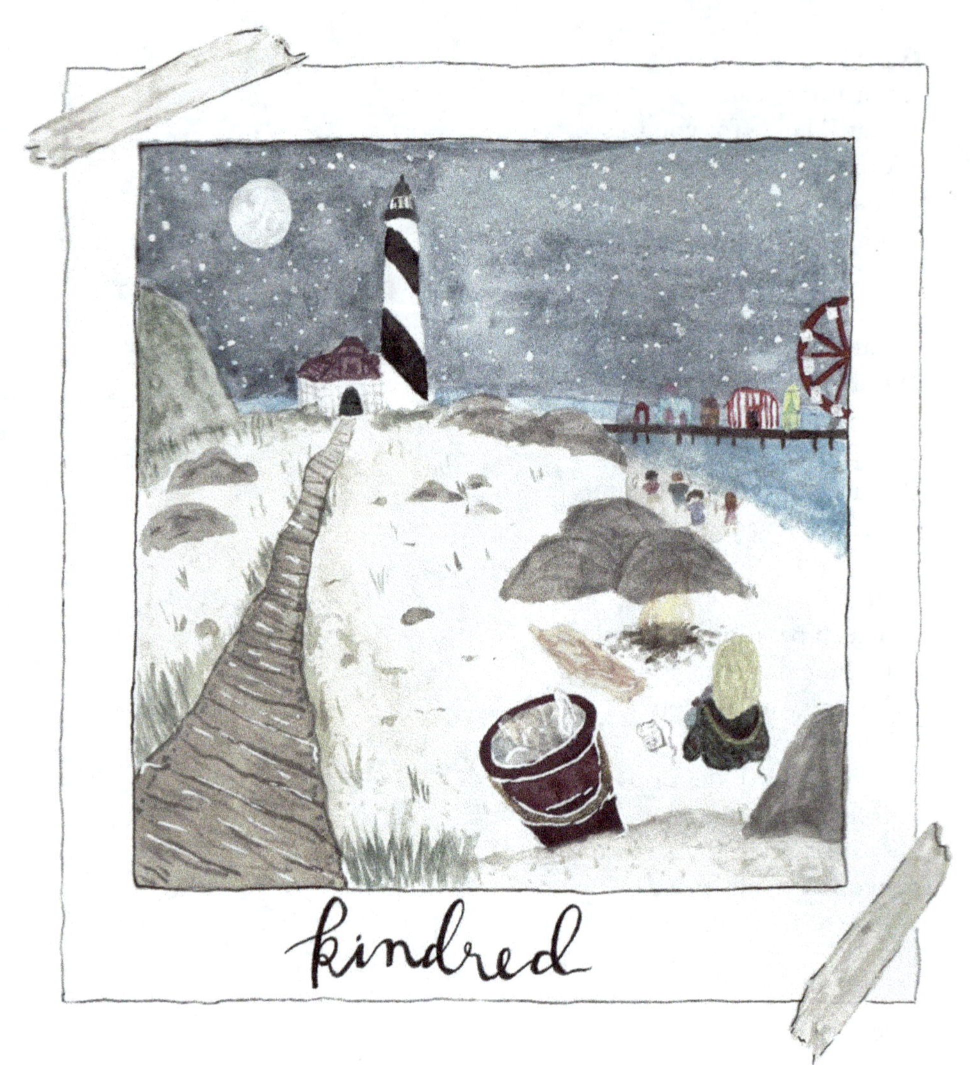

kindred

Kindred

Verse 1
I heard the words, "Come, join us!"
From a hearty bunch
By the water around dusk

We fell in step along the shore
Among friends now
No need to be troubled anymore

Their eyes glowed and glistened
As the moon began to shine
Forever friendly ears to listen

Wool sweaters and life partners
Swindled my scars
When they kindled my heart

Chorus
I wouldn't wish to walk this shore
With any companions in the world
But those my soul remembers as good friends
They share their memories and their shells
And care to know more than if I'm doing well
Their sincerity never ends
Like these yellow sands
I treasure those that are kindred

Verse 2
We snuck into the lighthouse
Shared our stories and jokes

Learned to tackle fears, learned to bouse

Ran to the boardwalk
Wasted time on games and rides
Stargazed while we talked

A suggestion for a quick midnight swim
Heard about their aspirations and introspections
The deeper we went, the more I wanted in

Carefree nonchalance and trusted confidants
Swindled my scars
When they kindled my heart

Chorus

Bridge
Together we wandered
Back to the shore
Together we pondered
If this night could last forevermore
As we sat around the fire
One thought lingered
In my mind
I've never felt so known, at ease, at peace
All my life

Chorus

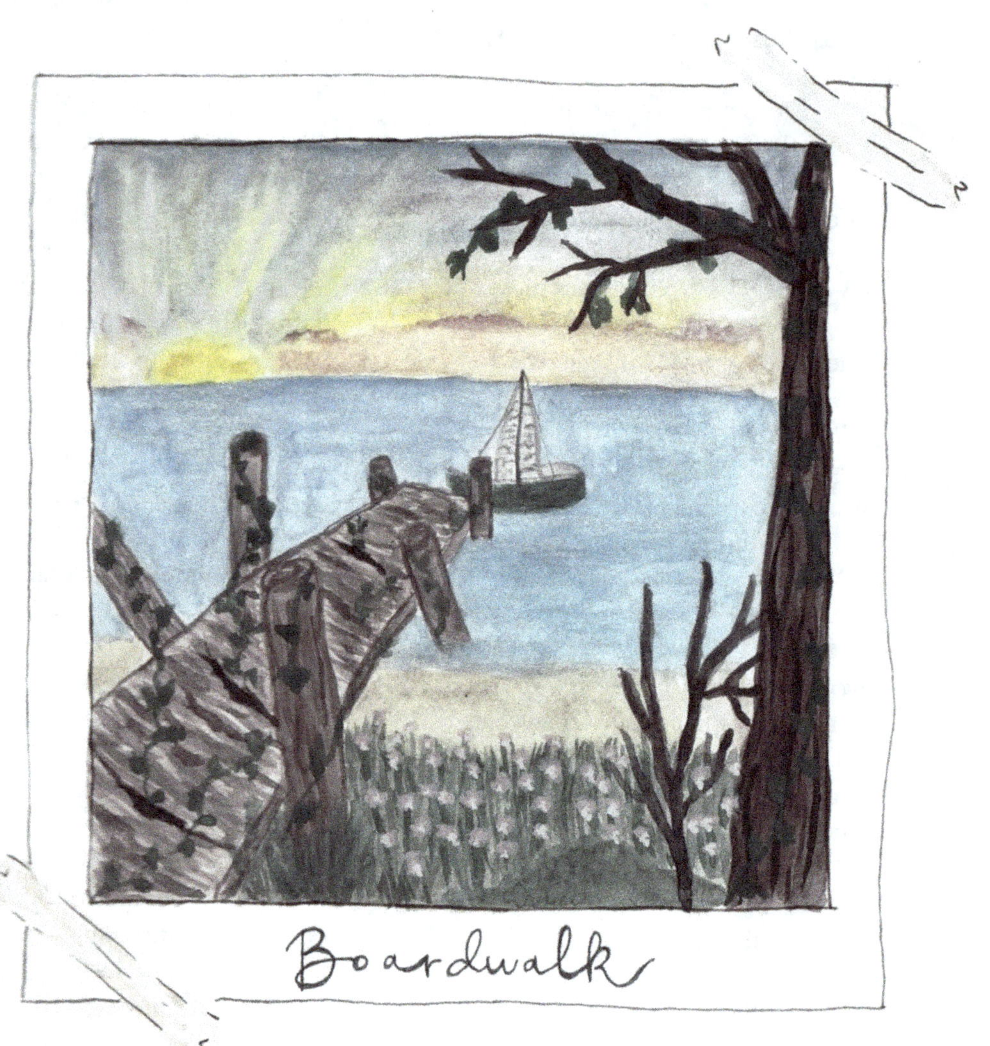

Boardwalk

Boardwalk

Verse 1
A flower squeezed
In the palm of a hand
A child's mind
Pure and innocent
Fragile like the boardwalk
Where I stand

Verse 2
I could stay, keep skipping rocks
Right off this boardwalk
Hope the rotting boards
Break no more
But the fragility inside me
Needs space to breathe

Verse 3
If I leave
Will those that are kindred to me
Promise there's always more
And they'll be waiting on the shore
For my return
From going out on the sea
To create, think, and process my feelings?

the work of God what is seen was made things that are not By Faith visible.

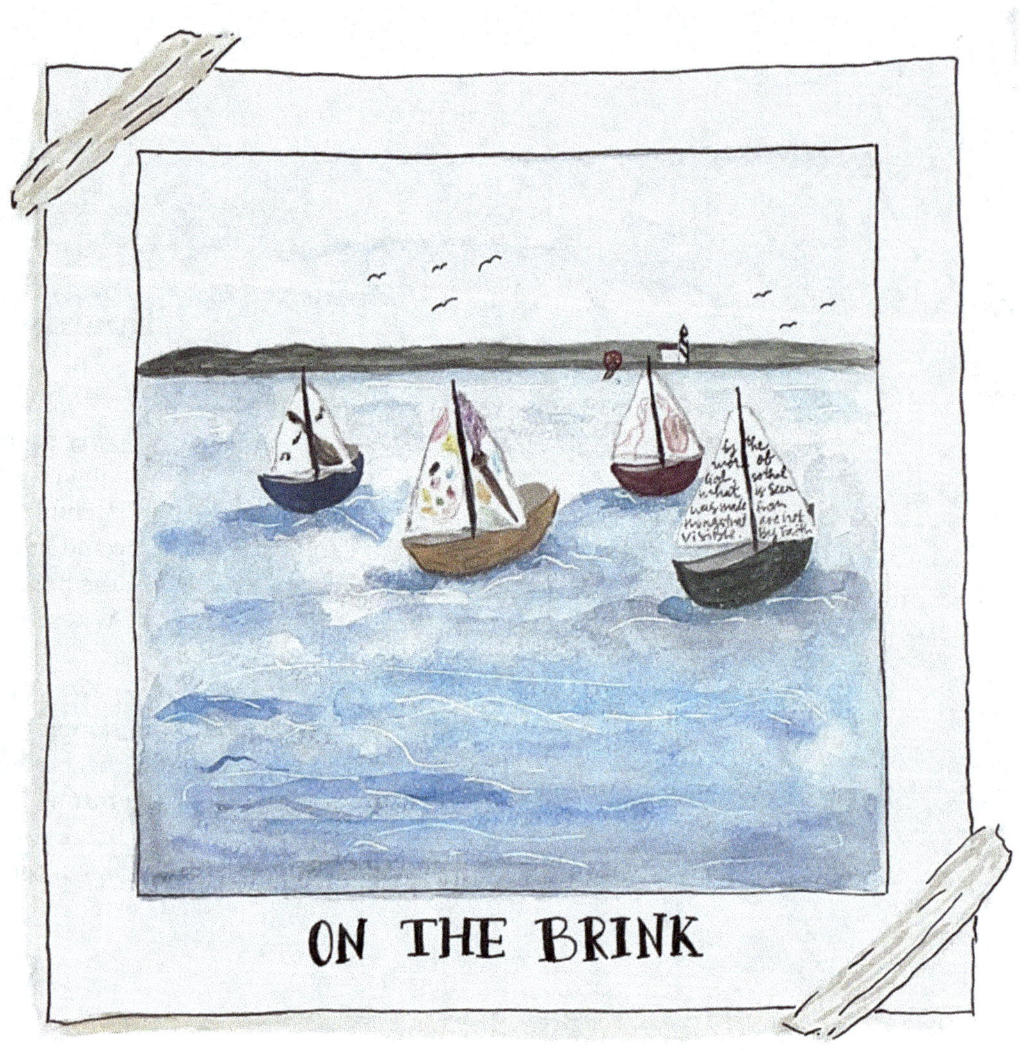

ON THE BRINK

On the Brink

Verse 1
A chill in my bones is
To harness the thrill
Waves crashing on
Open golden horizons
With the exhilarating rush of a pen
Riding a sea
Of creative possibilities

Pre-chorus
I look out over the sea and see
Other idealists, daydreamers, and
visionaries
Breathing the same liberating
Fresh air as me

Chorus
We look out over our starboards
To see all the stars abroad
Our helm guiding direction
Over the sea, our boats heeling
We tack and we jibe
Windward and leeward
Our point of sail
Is towards the air that makes us
feel alive

Verse 2
Mainsails in paint
Some covered in words
Some sway to rhythms
Others whistle melodies
Off the bow and the stern
Riding a sea
Of creative possibilities

Pre-chorus

Chorus

Bridge
Crossing every water
To kindle the fire of our desire
As it gets stronger
It swindles painful weals on keels
The wind dances through our hair
To keep it, we'd go anywhere
Chasing innovations through
creations
We won't sink constantly on the
brink

Chorus

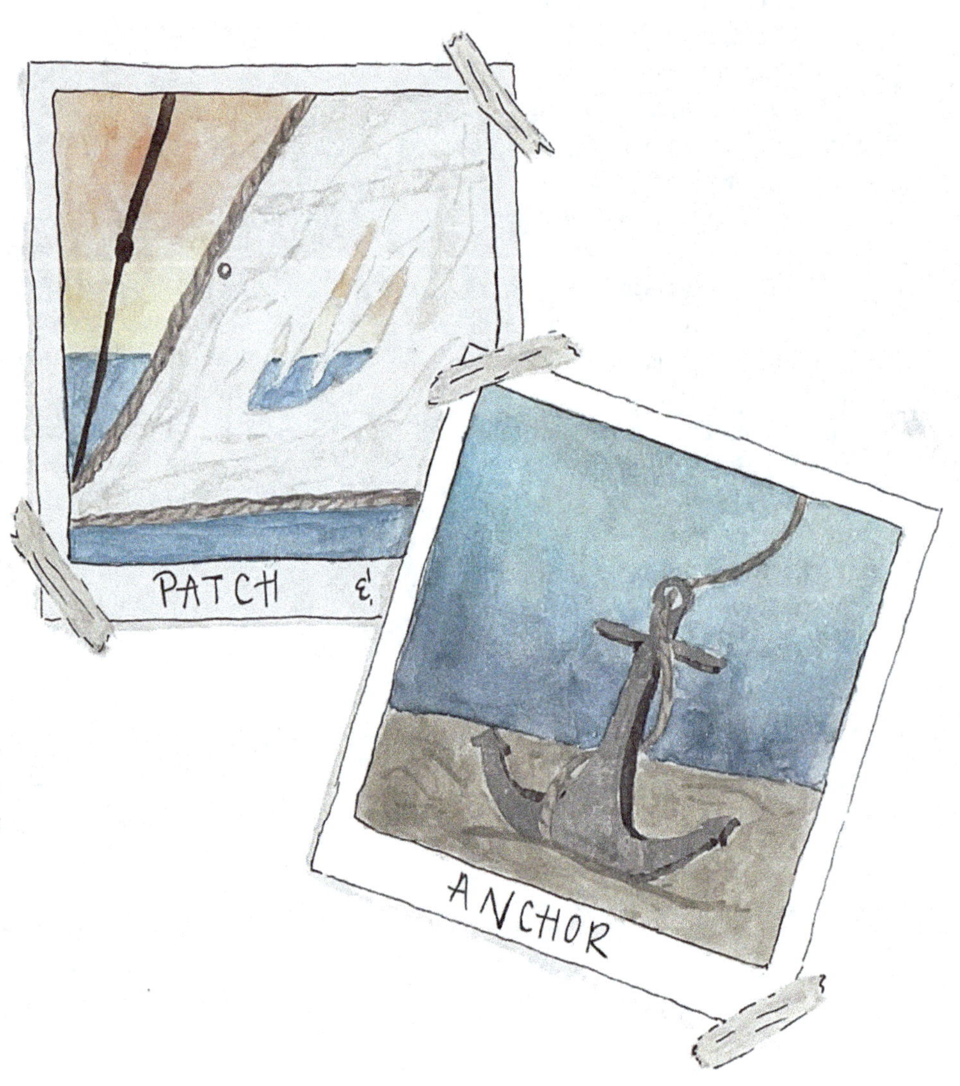

PATCH &
ANCHOR

Patch

Chorus
All I needed was a patch
On my sail
To know the rocking wouldn't last
But it was to no avail
You let time pass
And watched me fail
I walked on glass
Checking every detail
"Is there grace?" I needed to ask
I never could tell

Anchor

Chorus
I tossed about
Found by an anchor
Steadfast and no droughts
Of needed answers
Waves crashed up and down
But no longer unsure
Transformed inside out
To the core
Grace, not a doubt
The anchor assures

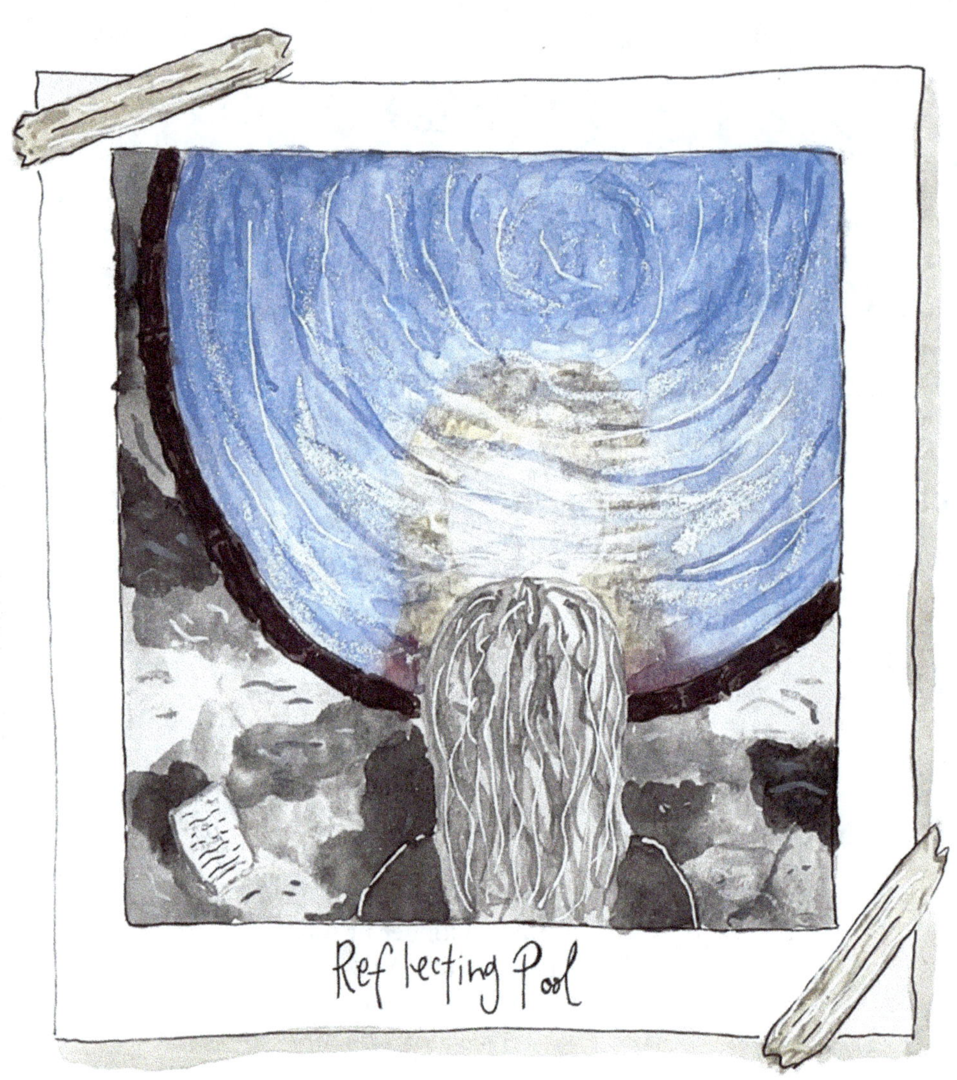

Reflecting Pool

Reflecting Pool

Verse 1
Regalia on my heart
Instead of on my head
Should be enough
Should be content

As its jewels gleam
Designed with depth
Full of value, meaning
And significance

Chorus
But as I look in the water
At my reflection
I see a pursuit of rarity
Full of desperation

Verse 2
Shells made of spires
Tapered with words
I collect in the pool
To give my reflection worth

Dreams bedizened in
Silver and gold
Tossed into the water
But fleeting efforts they hold

Chorus

Verse 3
I futilely fabricate
Trees lining a rose flushed sky
A pairi-daēza so ornate
As a backdrop

Meant to accentuate
My plain reflection
No one has the time to give it
attention
As it lasts for only an instance

Chorus

Bridge
So I pour my water colors into the
pool
Just like I color my world to give it
life
Skipping flashlight beams over the
water
Just to try to make it prismatic
another time
But it stays the same
It all fades away
I stand wondering
Will I always feel so empty
When the water reflects only me

Chorus

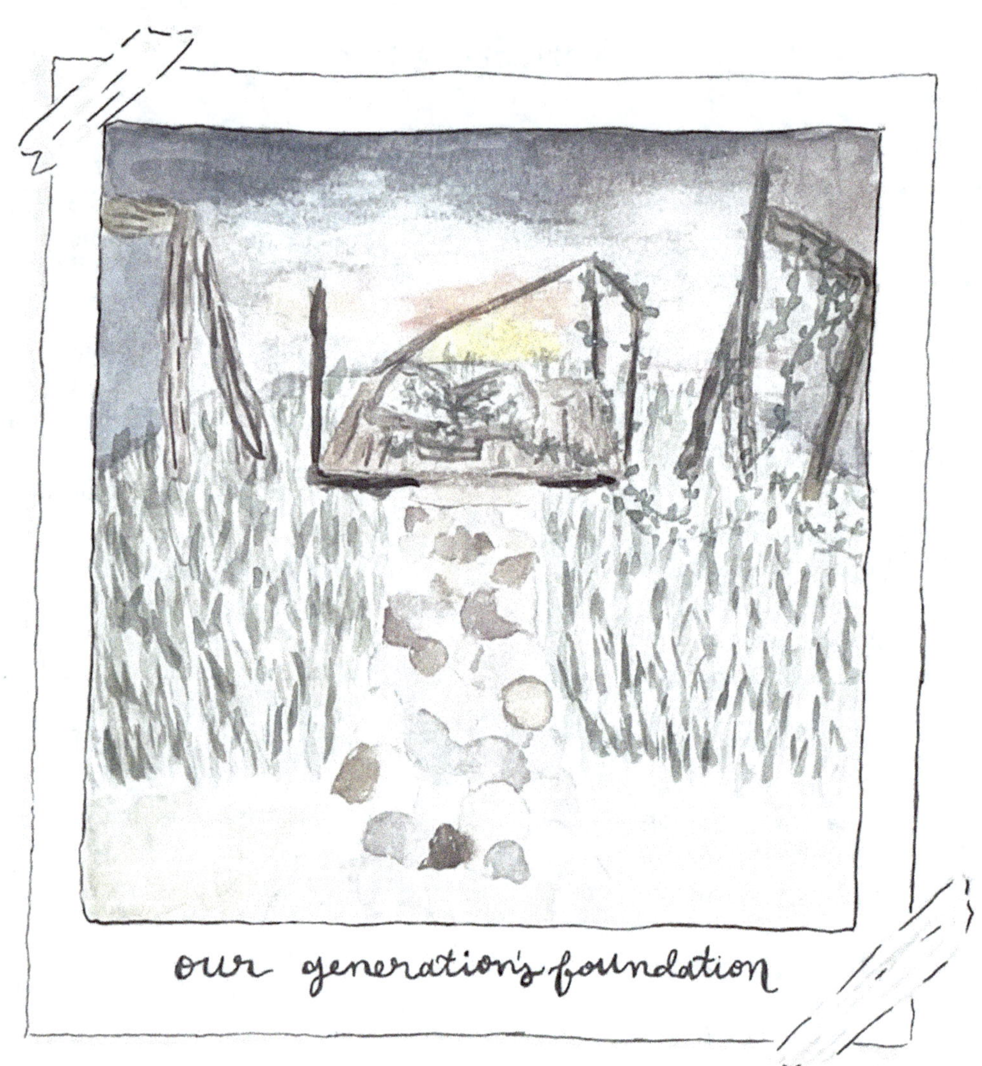

our generation's foundation

Our Generation's Foundation

Verse 1
A girl who builds
With blocks
A boy who paints
With colors
Will one day build paths to walk
Will one day paint art to discover
Their curious eyes
Blank canvas minds
Innocence, purity
Neglected and destroyed

Verse 2
As we argue
Over colors, red or blue?
Debates and brawls
Over the line leader
But with the line
In chaos
We are at more of a loss
If this is the world
We will pass on

Verse 3
The next generation
Future doctors, artists, and
teachers
Future politicians, parents, and
preachers
Turn on their TV's
To learn their ABC's
Instead they learn
Injustice, inequality, and
inhumanity
And count riots, divisions, and
hostilities
Before they can count to 3

Verse 4
Learning shouldn't stop
When we're handed a diploma
We intentionally cause call drops
Refusing to listen to other cultures
We shun, cancel, and exclude
Those who say, "I think differently
than you."
Yet
Still expect our children
To obey the golden rule

Verse 5
A boy told, "You're not listening."
by his mother
After witnessing her cancel another
A girl told, "Jesus came to save
your soul."
After seeing his name on the flags
rioters hold
How dare we
Teach our children falsely
Their nation, politics, or culture
Take priority in their identity

Verse 6
We will never be fair
In our ideals and beliefs
If all they do is
Make us enemies
We could have a million victories
But they amount to nothing
Placed next to our most tragic
failure of all:
Passing on the blueprints of a
delicate, disintegrated foundation
To our wide-eyed younger
generation

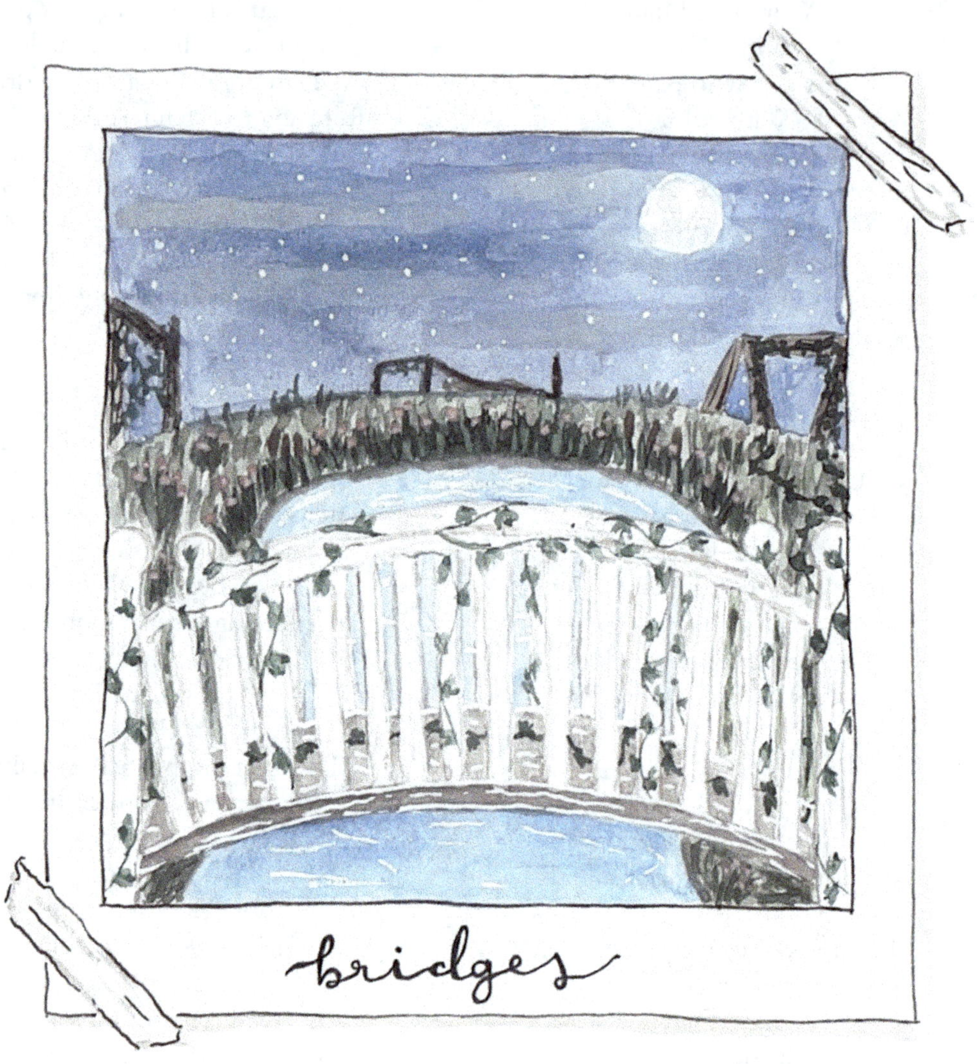

bridges

Bridges

Verse 1
What if we built bridges
Instead of taking sides
Formed joining paths
Instead of making divides

Verse 2
I look up, right is right
But when I cross the hill
The left becomes right

Verse 3
A simple change in perspective
An oxymoron, both objective and subjective

Verse 4
An acuity for unity

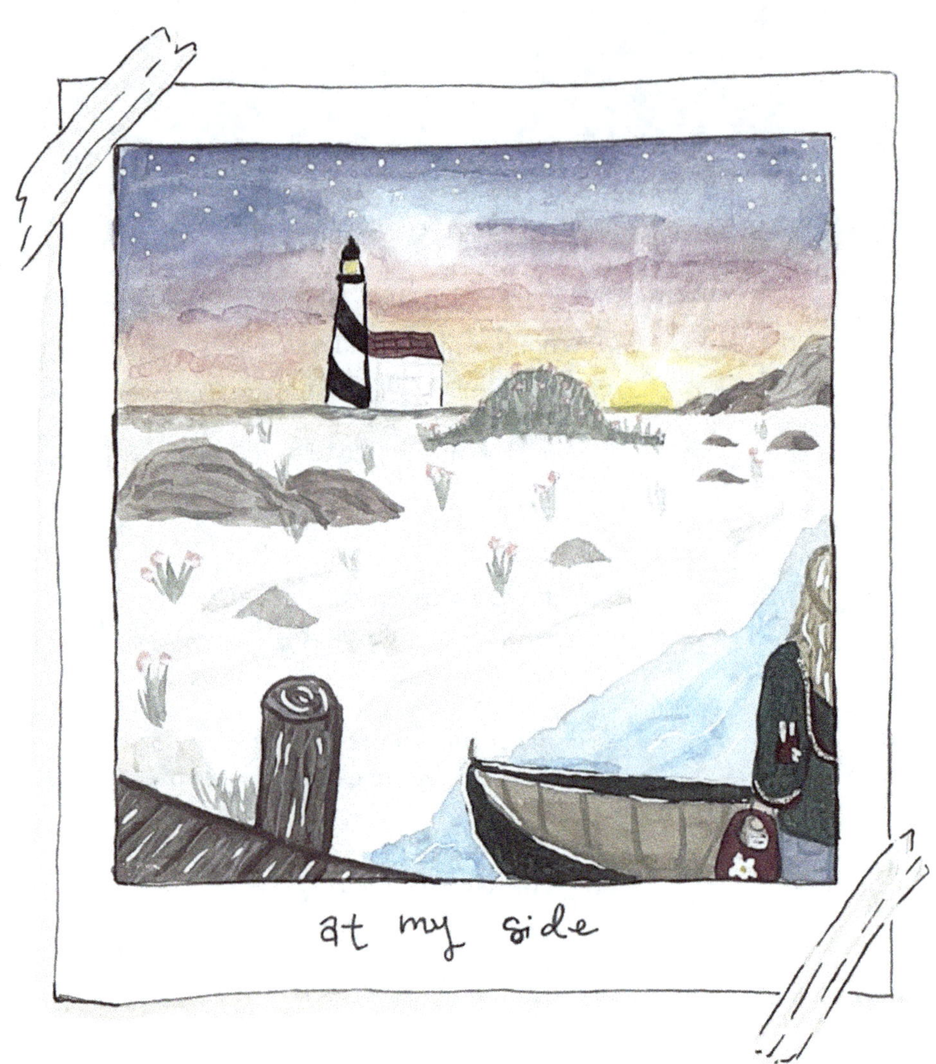

at my side

At My Side

Verse 1
Growing up with a variety
Of imaginative dreams
Of who I wanted to be

But through my days, looking ahead
There was one that led
The common thread

Chorus
Just shells in the sand
With no purpose
Until I collected them in my hand
With undeniable sureness
They turned into pens
And paper and words
Into more inspiration than I can control
Kept in my bag at my side
On the way to my treasure trove

Verse 2
Now I think in colors
Rhymes and iambic pentameter
Alliteration and tetrameter

I read Twain in my spare time
154 sonnets to clear my mind
Listen to Swift melodies to pass time

Chorus

Bridge
Coffeeshops on dreary
And rainy days
A new city to
Explore for a day
Hearing your hopes
for "One day…"
Makes me write today

Chorus

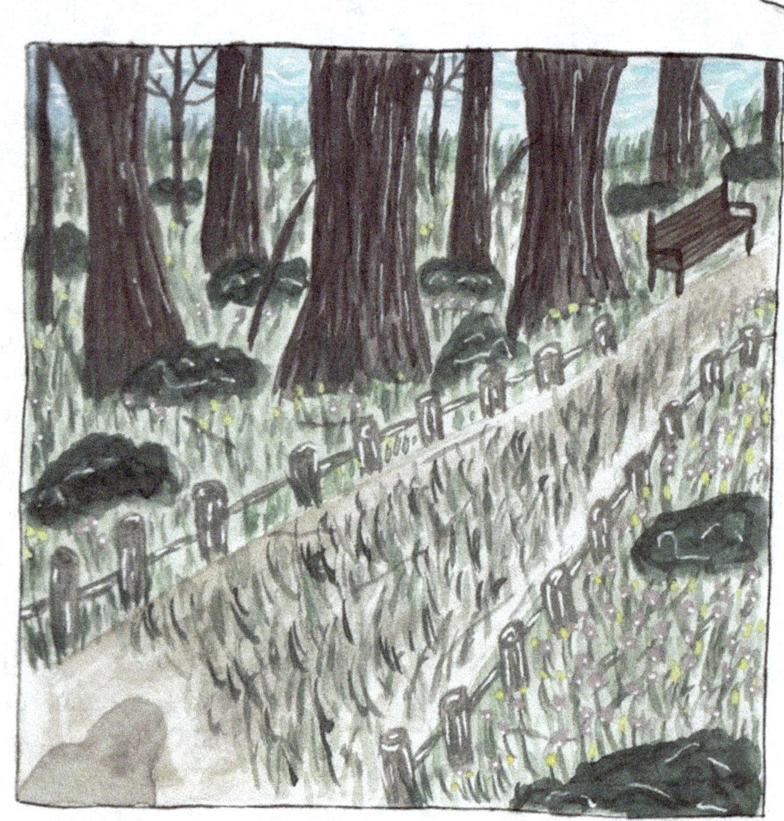

THE GRASS ON MY PATH

The Grass on My Path

Verse 1
There's grass on my path
It's been there awhile
I linger then walk past
As if the journey down it
Isn't worthwhile

Verse 2
Instead I opt for cheap treasures
Eventually slipping from my hand
I desperately grasp each one
But they fall away like sand

Verse 3
When I begin to question
My identity and worth
Every act that brings applause
Is what I frantically try to remember

Verse 4
Would I be as harsh and criticizing to someone else
As I am to myself?
Would I find something that lasts
If I just walked my path?

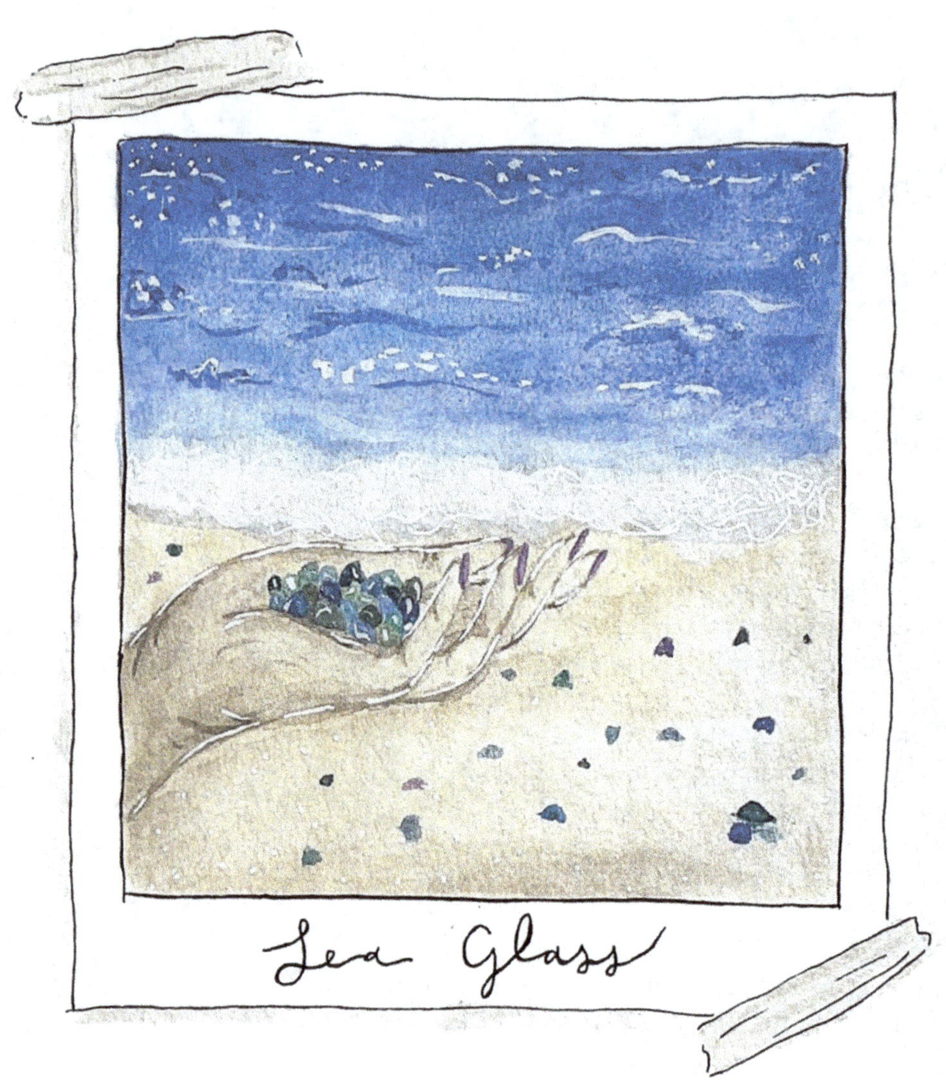

Sea Glass

Sea Glass

Verse 1
I hold sea glass
Collected over the years
Possible perceptions and assumptions
Ring in my ears

Their fragility echoes
In my mind
One misstep, mistake, misinterpretation
I fear I'll be seen in the wrong light

I think about what is true
Honorable, just, pure, lovely, commendable
But to perfectly practice such things
I've proven futile

Verse 2
One thing I've learned
One thing I know as truth
My witness is fragile
But the last word isn't found in what I do

It is found in Christ
Who is the everlasting word of life

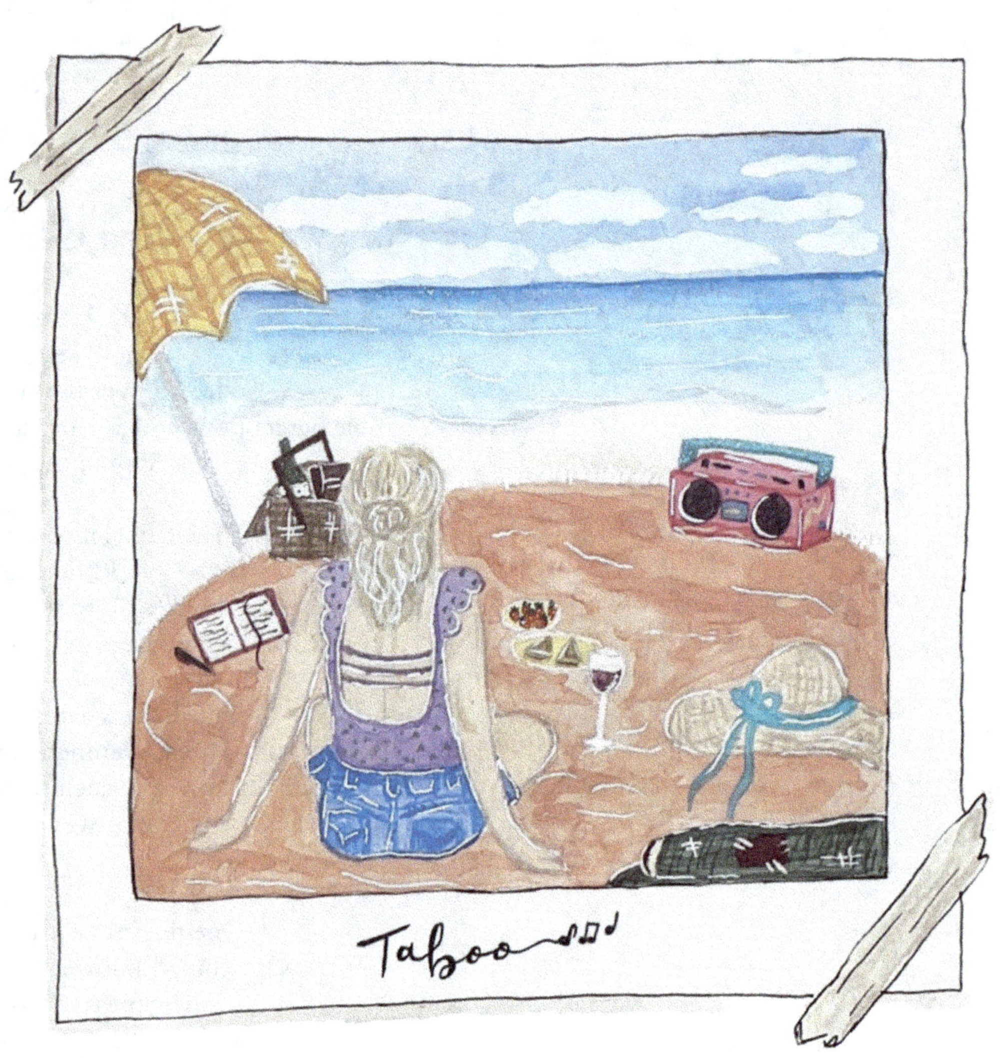

Taboo

Taboo

Verse 1
On a hot summer day
At Panama Beach
She strutted through the sand
Took a seat by the sea

She turned up the volume
On a hot pink stereo
Blaring 80's music
As she watched the people
Go by

Pre-chorus 1
And one by one
They gave her the side eye
Just like the people who told me
I feel too deep
And said I waste my time and energy
Crying over the silliest things

Chorus 1
It's taboo
Not acceptable to do
If you throw sand
They'll scold you
If one little thing seems off
They'll say that's your flaw

Verse 2
So she ate her sandwich
And drank her wine
Read a banned book
While the sun hung high

And when she got bored
She turned the music up more
Jumping and dancing
Not one beachgoer could ignore

Pre-chorus 2
And one by one
They moved, left her alone
Just like the people who told me
I think too deep
And said I waste my time and energy
Connecting too many unconnected
things

Chorus 1

Bridge
Intentionality over productivity
Finding significance in the ordinary
It's taboo, they ask how could I
choose
Things so ridiculous to do
But I took my seat by the sea
With my golden stereo
And turned my music up more and
more and more

Chorus 2
I'm a taboo
And I like what I do
Yes, I feel deep
And think deep too
Each little thing that's a piece of me
Makes a unique masterpiece

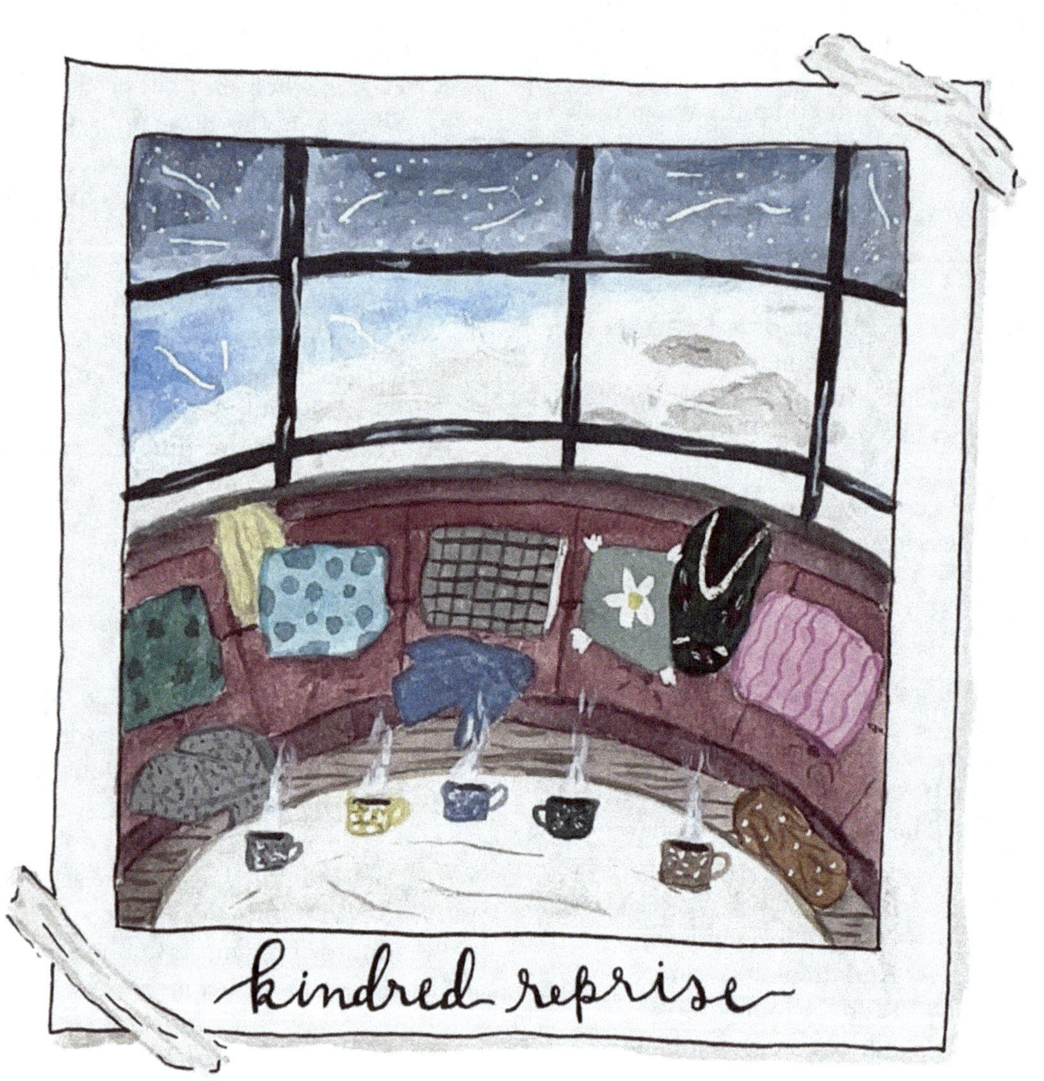

kindred reprise

Kindred Reprise

Verse 1
I hear the words, "Come join us!"
Echo in my mind
Doubting I'll hear them aloud another
time

I wander the shore alone
Arrive at the lighthouse by myself
Suddenly someone yells,

"We saved you a spot!"
On the beacon are my kindreds
Waving at me, greeting with grins

Wool sweaters and life partners
Swindled my scars
When they kindled my heart

Chorus
I will forever walk this shore
With the companions in this world
That my soul remembers as its
beacons
We share our memories and our shells
Whether we're all blue or doing well
Their sincerity never ends
Like these yellow sands
My treasure, those that are kindred

Verse 2
They saved me a spot

Share new jokes to share new laughs
We celebrate there's no more grass on
my path

They say that I was missed
While out at sea
And they waited to share a harvest of
peace

Dependable, steady, consistency
These are the ones
I've built trust on

Carefree nonchalance
And trusted confidants
Swindled my scars
When they kindled my heart

Chorus

Bridge
We pass around coffee another time
As we pass around elated smiles
I let out a peaceful sigh
Knowing they would be there for
miles and miles
As we sat around the fire
One thought lingered
In my mind
With these friends,
These kindreds,
I'll be known, at ease, at peace
All my life

Chorus

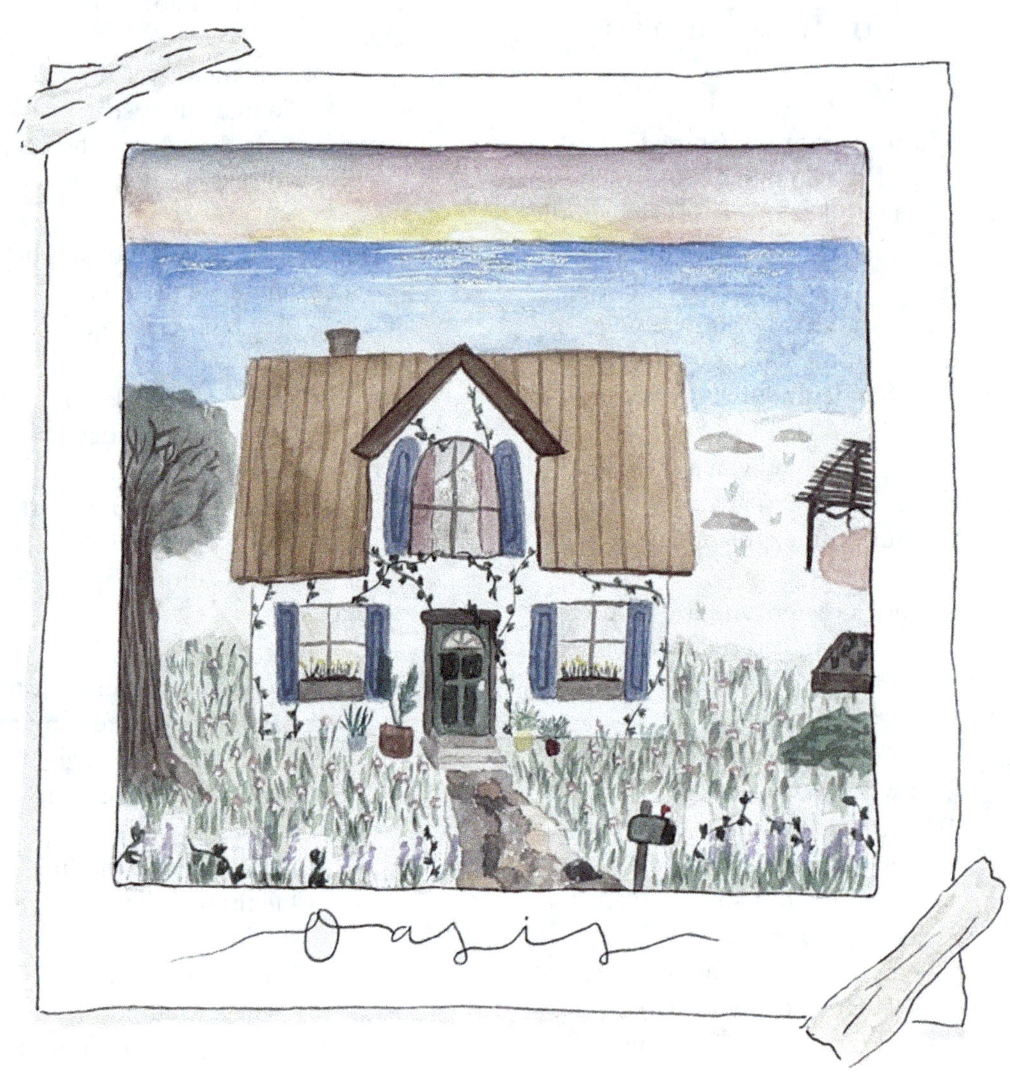

Oasis

Oasis

Verse 1
I muse on the melodic remedy
Strings that string my words on tapestry
It echoes as the shutters shutter in the wind
Windows built to weather violent storms
A golden light pouring out from within

Chorus
My oasis fabricated
On stilts of pathos
Framed by sung melodies
Stockinette stitches of prose
Long nights and early mornings
Starlight and sunlight
Ballads dance through the halls
Composing artistry on the walls
By candlelight I laugh, ponder, and cry
While days and nights sail by

Verse 2
The twain of thinking and feeling deeply
Rooted, growing along the wooden walls
As knitted ivy, kindling my homeland
Shades of jade, emerald, and verdelite swindle the nemeses within
Kept warm by a sweater on my shoulders and pen in my hand

Chorus

Bridge
Whether drought or storm
Continuous and laborious work
To protect what I adore
And not let this story end
As the water meets the shore
I retreat in again and again
Words, memories creviced in wooden floors
Harbor with an arbor of metaphors

Chorus

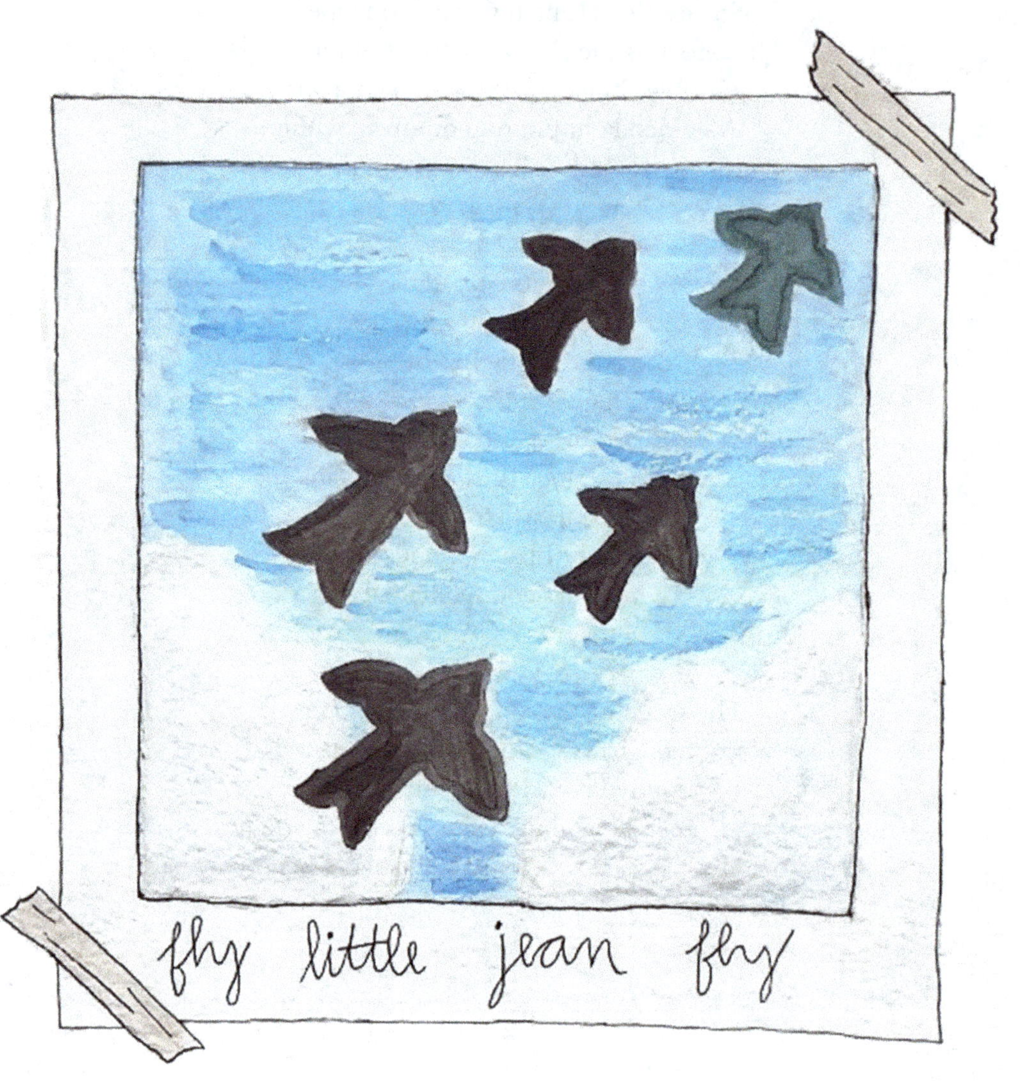

fly little jean fly

Fly Little Jean Fly

Verse 1
Seen perched on her treasure trove
Heart woven with words
Pen in neb
Tangled like a web
Her muse a melody
Echoing like a remedy

Verse 2
Fearlessness glistens in her eyes
As she espied the starlit skies
Trepidation disdained
Her only intent to evade
Escape by embracing her inner self
Feet fly to her harvest land

Verse 3
The ones who are kindred wait
They anticipate
For their beloved soulmate

Verse 4
From nest to neverland
She found her own sand
No more broken wings
Seen resting on her swing

Verse 5
Flock together
Wings spread
Pointed north
Ready to soar
Oasis bound

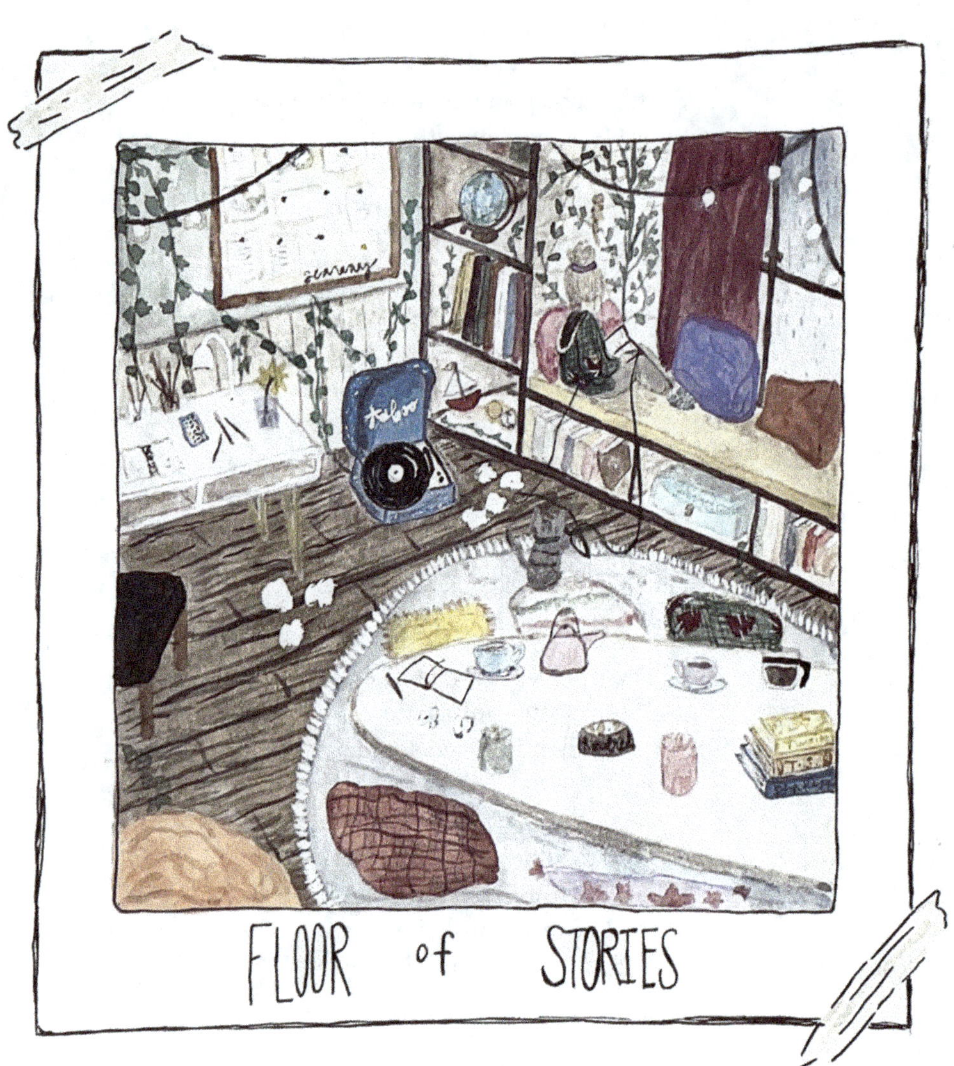

FLOOR of STORIES

Floor of Stories

Verse 1
Light barefoot steps
Creak wooden stairs
Carrying me to where
There is an air of nonchalance
With creative confidants
Time is nonexistent
Fears aren't persistent
I sip a cup of coffee
I slip into poetry

Chorus
And can't help myself
When an old record plays
Inspiration from the shelf
Of memories I've made
Candle flickers and scattered papers
Form the path for sparks
To flow from one to the other
And enliven us with our arts
We share tales and lores
Within four walls,
our camaraderie soars

Verse 2
Light streaming
On the mess of a desk
On palettes brushes and paint rest
There is a warmth of trust
With creative confidants
Peace is in existence
Empathy is persistent
They sip a cup of tea
They slip into painting

Chorus
And can't help themself
When an old record plays
Inspiration from the shelf
Of memories they've made
Candle flickers and scattered papers
Form the path for sparks
To flow from one to the other
And enliven us with our arts
We share tales and lores
Within four walls,
our camaraderie soars

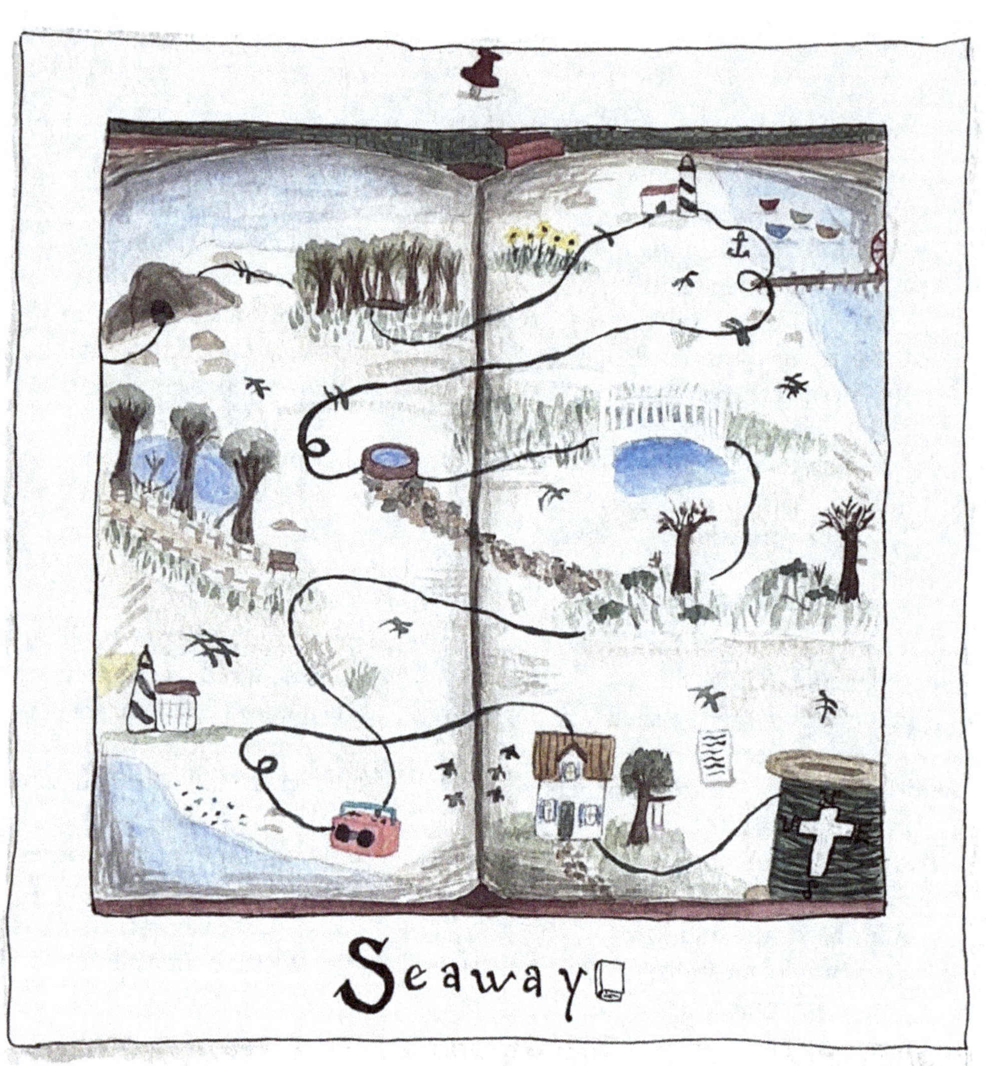

Seaway

Seaway

Verse 1
A story without an end
Because of a calm assurance
Paths of life form a map
I can walk with my pen

Verse 2
My anchor holds tomorrow
In his hand
Whether joy or sorrow
I live because he lives

Verse 3
The unknown still brings fear
My insecurities still ring ears
But I add more pieces to my map
Day by day
Because I know the one
Who navigates the way

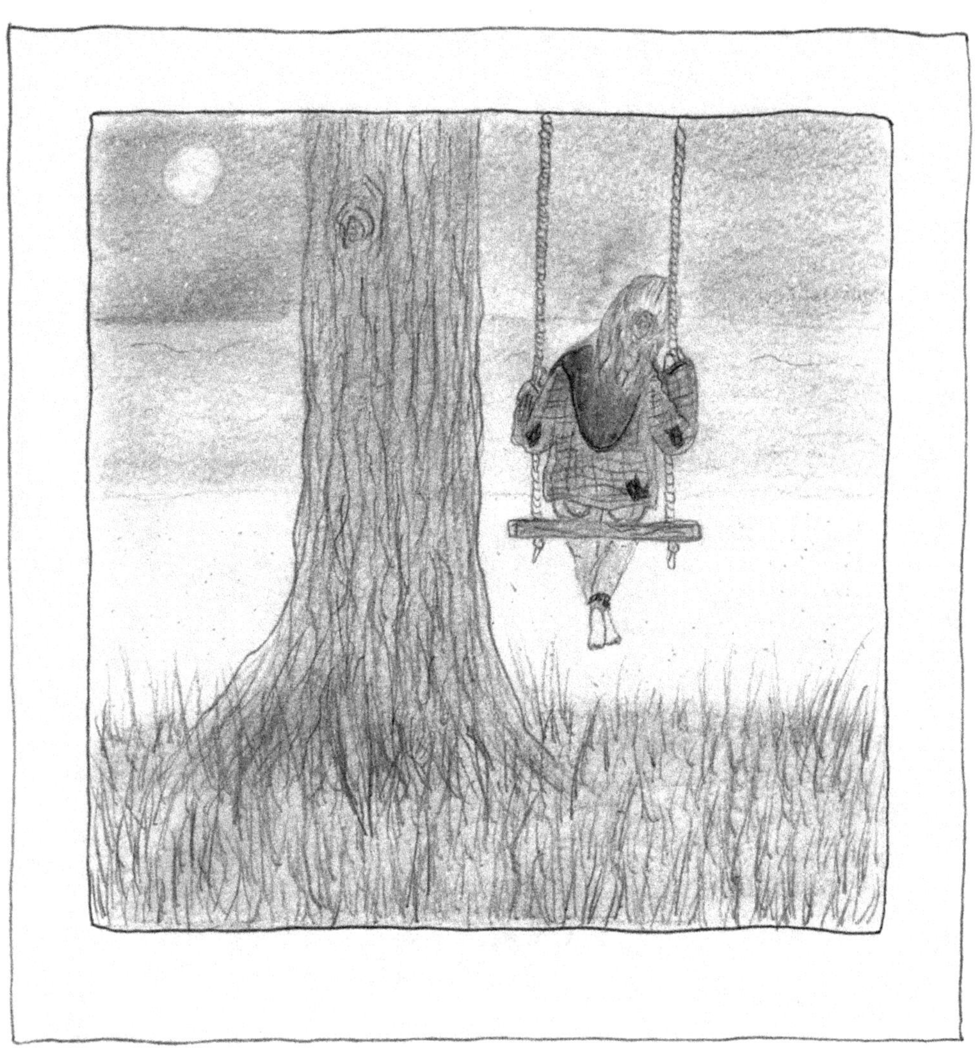

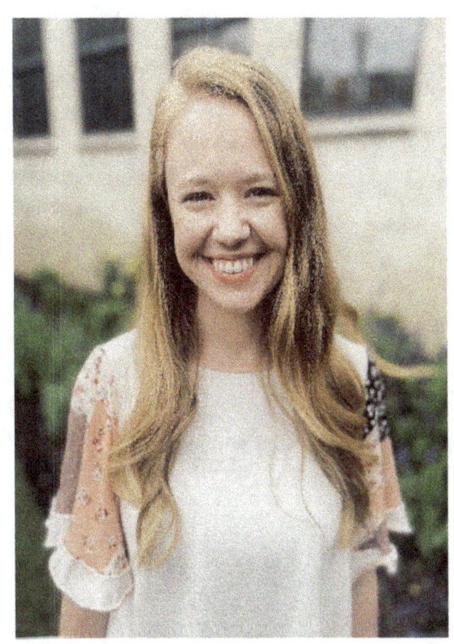

SAVANNAH GREEN

Savannah Green is the author of Seaway. She earned her Bachelor of Science in Education from Delta State University in 2019. Savannah is a current seminary student pursuing a Master of Divinity focusing in World Christianity and Witness. Her writings have been published by *Eight Hundred Words* and *Windrose Magazine*. She is also the founder and editor of *A Common Thread*, a website representing a community of artists. Savannah also shares her writing on her website *Words in the Crevice*. Her second poetry book, *Oasis*, is available on Amazon. When she isn't writing, Savannah enjoys visiting coffee shops, reading books, traveling to new cities, antique/thrift shopping, and spending time with her pets, Jemma and Fitz.

A Common Thread: acommonthread2.wixsite.com/community

Words in the Crevice: wordsinthecrevice.blogspot.com

Instagram: @savygreen

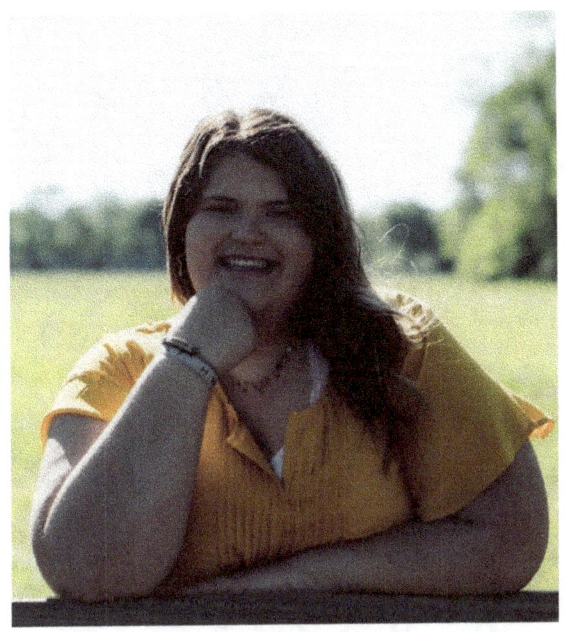

GRACE SPIVEY

Grace Spivey is the illustrator of Seaway. She earned her Bachelor of Science in Education from Delta State University in 2020. Grace is currently pursuing a Master of Elementary Education from Delta State University and is teaching 5th grade English. Art has always been a passion that has given her an escape to create. On the side, she sells custom watercolor illustrations for family, friends, and others. She contributes illustrations to *A Common Thread*. In her free time, Grace loves listening to her vinyls, watching Delta sunsets, taking long drives, and making memories with her kindreds.

A Common Thread: acommonthread2.wixsite.com/community

Instagram: @amazing_grace985

Art Instagram: @amazing_gracedesigns